When the Music Stops
A Mother's Journey in Crisis, Trauma, Grief & Loss

Debra L. Spears

Nellie Walker
May your bold testimony
shine a light piercing the
darkness.
Minister Debra L. Spears
2-18-13

ISBN: 1500858773
ISBN-13: 978-1500858773

DEDICATION

I dedicate this book to the love of family. My Grandmother Alice Hashaway Whittenberg raised me to value my family. To value all of the family's history, its failings and its successes. To value the love that binds us together one heart to another. To recognize we are all human. We need to stand with one another. Whether it is good, bad or ugly, we are united in our heritage. Alice was my singing Grandmama. Her love was in her nurturing spirit. I am the sum total of who I am because of who she taught me to be: A Strong Woman of God. Her legacy was the unconditional love of Christ.

To my children: my first born son, Devin Todd Hamilton (deceased), my middle daughter Nakisha Lynette Abernathy Carr (Bobby Carr), to my baby girl Kelli Latrese Abernathy. To my most precious grandchildren; Devin Todd Hamilton II, Alyssa Keleigh-D'von Hamilton, Bobilyn Giszelle Carr, Noah Amiel Carr and Kamryn Latrese Abernathy-Wynn. I also include my special grandsons Dominic Luper and Dajon Luper. To the newest member, my great-granddaughter Amiina Luper.

To all my siblings from my Mother Hilta Whittenberg Spears Jenkins (deceased): Denise L. Spears (deceased), Dawn L. Spears Osborne and DeCarla L. Jenkins Steele.

To all my siblings from my Father Vernon Harrison Sr. (deceased) and my Heart Mother Cecil Mae Harrison (deceased): Brenda Williams, Vernon Harrison Jr., Kim Baker McCray, Vernita Harrison Jackson, Laverne Harrison, Verna LaShawn Harrison and Vernado Harrison.

A special dedication in tribute to the memory of two special family members. First to my first cousin JoAnn Whittenberg who per her Mom was a heart of gold that stopped beating. This beautiful young woman was an identical twin. JoAnn was loved beyond measure. She was with us from February 6, 1960 to April 19, 1995. JoAnn was counted as one of the Oklahoma City bombing victim in the Alfred P. Murrah Federal Building. She worked in the Department of HUD on the seventh floor.

Second, to my sister Denise L. Spears who was 13 months my junior. She was the rising star of the family. We were blessed with her life from February 19, 1955 to March

9, 1998. She achieved the rank of Warden for the State of Oklahoma Department of Corrections with 20 years' service at the time of her passing. I wrote this poem for her service in appreciation of what she meant to each of us.

You Were Loved

The time came far too swiftly; it was so hard for us to part;
Your sweet smile we do remember in our heart of hearts.
We count God's many blessings,
Cause he loaned you for a time;
To his purpose you did surrender, and that made you shine.
You lived your life completely, as Mother,
Daughter, Sister, Aunt and Friend;
So we temper our sadness just until we meet again.
We cherish your goodness, we honor your strength
We are proud of your accomplishments
and all that they meant.
Your life was so precious, that we knew we had to share
Many times you touched another,
many times you dared to care
God met his promise to you,
when he called you by name

Home to share his presence,

free of illness and pain.

Thank you for the loving gift,

you left us in your son

He is our joy, your legacy,

your hope in life to come.

The road you had to travel, you did not go alone

Jesus walked beside you and now you are home

So special and so priceless is this your perfect day

Reflections on the time you spent, Denise you did okay

On your behalf our family

is blessed with much from above

And we are encouraged daily for we know

that you were loved.

CONTENTS

ACKNOWLEDGMENTS

I would like to thank my daughter Kelli Abernathy for her invaluable assistance motivating me to complete this book. Her strategic marketing and implementation to help produce my story is outstanding. I would like to thank my friend of many years, Pastor Betty Neal for her ministry of delegation, inspiration, and motivation to get this book done. I would like to thank Krystal Wright for being one of the listening ears I needed to work on the editing of the book. I would like to thank Melodie Moore for being a faithful prayer partner, touching and agreeing during this time. I would like to thank my cohorts in the Clinical Pastoral Education (CPE) Program at OU Medical for working with me and challenging me through the tough cases. I would like to thank the long list of faithful friends who have encouraged and cared for me so compassionately. If I listed all the names I would run out of print. You know who you are and how valuable your love and friendship is to me. I hold you all in my heart.

CHAPTER ONE - I WAS NOT READY

The Music stopped for me at 4:30 A.M. on the morning of August 21, 2006. I was awakened by my daughter Kelli to come quickly. She said, "Devin's clock is going off. I went to see why it was still on. I tried to get him to wake up but I can't move him. Devin is down and he won't wake up!" "Devin is down" was our phrase when he would have a diabetic episode. His blood sugar would fall too low. He would be in crisis. I jumped up and ran quickly to his room. I realized instantly that this time would be different. We would dial 911. I could already see by the unnatural position in which he lay that all was not well, not this time.

Hear my prayer, LORD;
let my cry for help come to you.
[2] Do not hide your face from me when I am in distress.
Turn your ear to me;
when I call, answer me quickly.
Psalm 102: 1-2

Use Your Resources

My resources involved music. Music is a highly emotionally engaged reward system to the body that resides deep in the brain. Music activates the areas dealing with reward, motivation and emotion. Music became my first inclination to listen for God in his creation.

I recall my strongest memories are of waking every morning to birds chirping and singing. The sound of music in the air ringing in the new day was one of my greatest joys. The hustle and bustle of daily activities for me became the music of life. My grandmother Alice used to get up with the chickens. She would sing us up out of bed with her gospel songs, hymns and the smell of her hot food cooking on the stove.

Music became the prayer language of my heart. It was a way to bring me closer in my walk with God. Music introduced me to worship. Worship made my heart soar to the heights of heaven. Music made life make sense. Music was a resource for my soul. I could sing when happy. I would sing when sad. I tried to sing my heart out of any negativity or crisis that came my way.

How innocent and naïve I was. I didn't yet realize that it wasn't music that would sustain me in times of crisis. It is only through the love of God as the creator of the music would I overcome. He could teach me to lean and depend on him. I had no experience to prepare me for the times ahead. Those times that would bring pain so deep, so hard, so hurtful that I could not talk, walk, look up, sing or pray.

When I met death, I learned the song in my heart would stop. I didn't know how to deal with the spiritual disconnection. I had no understanding of the level of hurt and loneliness that took my song away. The times I could not meditate. The times I couldn't pray.

In The Beginning

Devin had a rough start in life. Born at 33 weeks he was jaundiced and weighed 6 lbs. 11 oz. Had Devin been born full term he was going to be a big baby. At his three week checkup he weighed 11 pounds. At his six weeks checkup he weighed 19 lbs. At three months old he weighed 22 lbs. His pediatrician put him on a diet of skim milk. As a young mother, I had no idea the signs and symptoms of diabetes. I had no idea the magnitude of the journey that lies ahead.

At age 12 months, Devin developed asthma and severe allergies. He had to have weekly allergy shots from age 12 months to age 24 months. His allergies were so severe; he couldn't have rugs or curtains in his bedroom. Everything was covered with plastic. His food choices were limited. He couldn't go outside for long periods of time even when the pollen count was low. Everything triggered an allergic reaction. I was out of my element. I began to pray.

Devin was diagnosed as a Type 1 diabetic at the age of 7. Diabetes struck without warning. This was my first life or death crisis as a mother. I wasn't prepared. I remember my son asking me at this young age, "Why did God make me different?" That was the beginning of our journey of faith together. What a challenge? We studied the Book of Job together. I had to break down scriptures in a way a 7 year old could understand. God gave us both the Gift of Faith and our belief in healing.

As Devin's body grew his diabetes would be in and out of control. He was called a brittle diabetic. I had never heard that term before. His blood sugars would spike at each growth spurt. He was in and out of Oklahoma City's Children's Hospital all the time. The family missed holiday celebrations, birthday parties, special events because Devin was in crisis. We could not plan anything. If we did we were guaranteed to have to cancel. To say that Children's Hospital was my second residence would be putting it mildly. Life in the family revolved around Devin and his medical needs. I prayed for my girls to have a normal life in spite of my son's needs.

Faith Is

Faith is the confidence that what we hope for will actually happen; it gives us assurance about things we cannot see.

Hebrews 11:1

The journey became complicated. From birth to age 11 Devin had medical insurance through my employment. However, He was uninsurable for life insurance. I worried what I would do should the unthinkable happen. Devin had delayed physical growth in the area of male issues. I was told Devin would never have children. I grieved the possibility that I may not have grandchildren from Devin. I clung to the hope that God still had the last say. I held on to the possibilities of grandkids through the girls when they got older.

I worked diligently with his medical doctors to regulate his blood sugars. Finally at the age of 13, I was able to get Devin a limited life insurance policy that would be all he had through his adulthood. It was a specialty policy through a diabetic group that could never be increased. At least he had something. I could mark that worry off my list.

Devin had major life struggles with diabetes. Many times he almost died. Many times God perfectly put things in motion for him to be revived over and over again. The odds were not good that his health could keep up. We worried about the long term damage to his body. I was fearful of all the complications that could happen with his illness. Some mornings Devin woke up and could not walk. The circulation was poor in his young legs. Sometimes he had problems seeing. He was diagnosed with diabetic myopathy. Every day was another hurdle. I thanked God for each new mercy.

The First Casualty

My marriage became a casualty of the long term wear and tear on the family. The responsibility of taking care of a child with long term medical needs was too heavy. There were added strains along with frayed nerves. We had different parenting styles. All of it contributed to the constant conflict between us. We both were committed to the girls having as normal life as possible around their sick brother.

It was no one's fault but it happened just the same. Love just wasn't enough to sustain the constant assault of emotions. One day my husband said he just didn't want to be married anymore. What can a wife and mother say to that? I loved him enough to let him go. I had bigger things on my plate. Jesus be a fence all around me.

As Real As It Gets

Now here we are with another crisis. Kelli was on the phone with 911 waiting to do what we always do to revive her brother. But I knew this was different. When I went into his room the light switch didn't work. Devin had turned the light off so he could run his ceiling fan during the night. The problem was the room was extremely dark. I had to feel my way into the room. I tried to do so without hitting my toe on his massive bed. I felt for the chain and pulled it. I wasn't ready for what I saw!

There he was lying on his stomach. His head was turned to the wall. I could see something was wrong. I looked at the back of his chest and saw no movement. I followed the line of his body back toward me. I saw his leg slightly elevated above the bed. I knew with every fiber of my being that his leg was in rigor. "Don't touch him. Just don't touch him and it won't be real." That's what my mind told my heart. My heart wanted to reach out and gently lay his leg down. But I just couldn't do it. That's how I found him. That's how he needed to stay until help arrived. Lord help me. Lord help me please!

Kelli is now talking on the phone with the 911 Operator. She was trying to make sense of the instructions. I know in my heart now that Devin is already gone. I've got to keep Kelli out of this room. I've got to tell her. There's no time to do it gently. I put my arm across the bedroom door. Kelli tries to come into the room. I won't let her past my arm. She is parroting what the 911 Operator is saying. She asked, "Is he breathing? I said as calmly as I could, "Tell them he's not breathing." It hit her like a ton of bricks. "He's not breathing", she asked? Softly I said "No, Kelli, he's not."

When I turned to look at her face she still had the phone gripped in her hand but it now down to her side. All I saw was those enormous round tears welling up in her eyes. I could hear the 911 operator on the phone saying "Hello, Hello". We just stood there silently together. For us time stood perfectly still. The morning was dead. There was no music. There was no sound at all.

At the moment of shock and awe, our minds record the sights, sounds, smells, touches, tastes we associate with the crisis or trauma. Music imprints in such a unique way that it connects the heart and mind together for instant recall of the event. When asked where you were when _____ happened? We are instantly catapulted into the event.

What songs when you hear them make you happy or sad? Is the event you remember also happy or sad? If sad, do you avoid even listening to that song? Do you turn the song off or change to another song the minute you realize what you are hearing? If so then your mind has married the event to the song. You need to work through the issues associated with the song to work through your grief.

I found that when the music stopped for me, I was actually imprinting the sounds, sights, smells and tastes associated with the event. They would become forever part of my remembrance process. They would be the memories that sustained me.

Reflections

1. In reading my story, what type of event are you remembering that still causes you the most pain: Crisis, Trauma, Grief or Loss?

2. Who was the person you are remembering?

3. What is their relationship to you?

4. List all the feelings about the event that you still hold near your heart today?

5. How long have you been carrying around this weight?

6. Are you open to sharing the details with someone safe to listen?

7. Who would you choose to share those details with?

8. Is there any rational reason you can't call them today?

9. Are you in panic? Breathe. You are going to be okay. Breathe in, out, slowly.

10. Do you have more than one event that you are remembering?
    If so, answer the same questions for each event. Write them down so you can review and refresh in your mind what happened.

CHAPTER TWO - THE STRUGGLE IS REAL

I was already circling the drain so to speak when the Death Angel came knocking this time. In order to fully understand exactly how traumatized I was, I need to go back two months. Two months of my life that altered my place in God's universe. Two months that redefined who I thought I was. Two months to figure out why am I here? What is my purpose in all this? God what do you want from me?

I won a once in a lifetime trip in a drawing. It was an all-expense paid trip for four, anywhere, anytime that year. Wow! I was ecstatic. The itinerary was to leave Oklahoma City on June 12th. Devin could not go. His health was not good. He couldn't leave the country due to his dialysis treatments. My daughter, Capt. Nakisha could not leave her Pastorate and church activities. She and her husband Capt. Bobby, and their two babies; Bobilyn aged 24 months and Noah aged 9 months were being re-assigned to a new church. The family was moving in three weeks. My kids were moving from South Carolina now 21 hours away. They were moving back to Oklahoma, Nakisha's home state. They would now reside one hour fifteen minutes straight up the Turner Turnpike in Sapulpa, Oklahoma.

My mom could not go. She had congestive heart failure. Mom was paralyzed on her left side for the last 10 years from a stroke. She could not endure the stress of a long trip. What if she got sick along the way? What if she, heaven forbid, got sick when we got there? Someone would have to stay behind. She'd be stuck in a foreign country. I could not take the chance. I didn't tell mom about us all leaving until the last possible minute. We made every preparation for her while we were going to be gone. I knew she would be hurt and disappointed but it was the right decision.

The solution was to take my youngest daughter Kelli and two of my sisters, Dawn and DeCarla, on the trip. We drove from Oklahoma City to Dallas to spend the night. The next morning we flew out of DFW Airport headed to Playa Del Carmen in Rivera Mexico. The trip was for five days and four glorious nights of all inclusive fun. The trip was almost uneventful. Dawn and I set off the security alarms. Dawn had a knee replacement. I had a lumbar fusion with five pounds of rods and screws in my lower back. After security used the wand on us we cleared customs. There were no other hitches to the trip. Finally, we were on our way.

A Change of Perspective

We arrived at the Cancun Airport. We traveled by Mercedes bus to the hotel in Playa Del Carmen. What excitement! What a mountain top experience for us. We ate. We shopped. We ate. We swam. We ate. We toured the area. We ate. We went para-sailing. We had to Jet Ski out to the waiting boat. After a brief training demonstration, we were hoisted up. DeCarla stayed on the beach. What a chicken! She decided to take pictures. Dawn and Kelli went up together. I went up alone.

While riding the para-sail, I could see all the way to Belize. I think the captain said we were 70 feet up. From that height I watched sea turtles swimming below. I could see God in his creation everywhere. How beautiful. How peaceful. The warm ocean breeze was like the breath of

God surrounding me. Time stood still. I wanted that feeling of being close to God to last. Most of all I wanted to hold on to the euphoric feelings. We had a fellowship of an all girls' week. It was both a spiritual and a perfect phenomenal high.

> What joy for those who can live in your house,
> always singing your praises.
> What joy for those whose strength comes from the LORD,
> who have set their minds on a pilgrimage to Jerusalem.
> Psalm 84:4-5

At last the days of fun in the sun were over. We retraced our trip back into the country. We had to re-enter the real world. We had to come home. Dallas was only a three and a half hour drive back to Oklahoma City. On the road trip back from DFW Airport to Oklahoma City, we called Mom from the car. She was so excited to hear all about the trip. She wanted to know if we brought her something back, always the kid. I assured her, we bought her the perfect dress. She was giving us a laundry list of things we needed to do for her when we returned. We were bubbling over with laughter. We were giddy retelling some of the events we experienced. We couldn't wait to share our trip and pictures with other family members. The trip was such a great success. What a blessing! Little did we know that the mountain top experience would be the resource we would need. We were about to face the impact of the valley we were entering together?

Walking By Faith

When they walk through the Valley of Weeping,
it will become a place of refreshing springs.
The autumn rains will clothe it with blessings.
[7] They will continue to grow stronger,
and each of them will appear before God in Jerusalem.
Psalm 84:6-7

The next morning my youngest sister, DeCarla found Mom slumped over in her chair unconscious and in distress. She called 911. She then called us, her two sisters. EMT's were whisking Mom to the nearest hospital. All night Mom was treated with such dignity and care. She was moved from the ER to ICU. We took turns sitting with Mom and reassuring ourselves. One of us was with her the entire time.

My Daughter Needs Me

I had problems. One problem was I needed to be with my Mom. The other problem; I was scheduled to leave out at midnight. I planned to drive the 21 hours solo to Rock Hill, South Carolina. I had pre-arranged to help my daughter and son in law load their moving truck. The Plan was to pack, sleep and clean the parsonage in Rock Hill the last few days before the move.

The family would then attend the final Sunday Services. They needed to say farewell to the church they had come to love. The church was ready to show their love back to them. Capt. Kisha would lead the final worship service. Capt. Bobby would preach his farewell sermon.

Our family had to take the final trip back to Oklahoma City. My son in law would drive the moving van. I would follow driving my daughter and two small grandkids in my car. As I said that was the plan. The best laid plans of mice and men, right? God saw things differently.

I had such high hopes that Mom would pull through. She always did every single time before. I just knew that she would stabilize. I could start out on the road later than desired. I would get less sleep on the other end. I could still make everything turn out right. But I had a feeling. Jesus what else can go wrong?

God let me sleep past my midnight alarm. I must have been tired. I called DeCarla who gave me the update that Mom was better. She was resting. After much reassurance I decided to head out to South Carolina at 8 A.M.

A curious thing happened on the road. My Crohn's disease was very active due to stress. The route from my house to Okemah, Oklahoma is normally a one hour trip. I had to stop at every exit with a restroom along the route. My stomach would not settle down. I knew I was having a hard time but I was determined to stay the course. When I came out of the last pit stop it was 10:00 A.M. The one hour leg had now taken me two hours. Then I got the dreaded phone call to get back to the hospital ASAP. Mom had taken a turn for the worse.

My Mom Needs Me More

When I tell you God has a hedge of protection around us, believe me it is real. I drove in excess of 80 miles per hour. I arrived back in the city limits in record time. While still fifteen minutes out, I got another call from my daughter Kelli crying now, "Hurry, please"! My car seemed to glide the rest of the way. I don't remember pulling into the parking lot of the hospital. I don't remember making my way back to ICU. What I do remember is walking in to see the crash team in the midst of a Code Blue working on Mom.

While waiting I kept looking so I could see her face. Mom was a stanch Christian. Yet, I knew she had an unnatural fear of dying. Every time she would go into the hospital with an emergency, a lone tear would slide down from the corner of her eye. I was looking for that tear. Finally, the crash team stopped working. I heard the doctor call out, "time of death 10:30 AM". The music stopped on July 21, 2006, my mother was gone and she had no tear.

Immediately from the family members came the loud roar of pain. The cries and moans of all the hurt, disbelief, shock and awe as the family huddled around the door of the room. We had to quickly move everyone out of ICU into the Family Comfort room. Comfort is really the last thing you feel in that room. The doctor came in and explained mom had coded five times. They could not bring her back. All the grandkids were devastated. Her girls were just numb. What now? What do we need to do next? For me there were no words. Shouldn't there be soothing music playing somewhere. Nothing, nothing but emptiness.

When crisis and loss happens, and it does happen to us all, what helps you to find your focus in the midst of your pain? What helps to comfort you? Do you need soft sounds to soothe you? Or, must you have quiet time? I had to go into my secret room, my prayer closet to regroup.

Reflections

1. Do you have a spiritual or religious community in times of crisis?

2. If not what other community resources are available to you?

3. Are they supportive to you?

4. Do you feel cared for by the community?

5. Is there one person or a group of people you really fit in with?

6. Are you able to let them help you work through your feelings?

7. Do you trust them to care for you unconditionally?

8. Do you feel your story is "safe" with them?

9. Have you re-engaged in external activities with your community?

10. Have you let people back into your inner circle?

CHAPTER THREE - I ALMOST LET GO

O LORD, how long will you forget me? Forever?
How long will you look the other way?
How long must I struggle with anguish in my soul,
with sorrow in my heart every day?
Psalm 13:1-2

The struggle to find clarity, purpose and the meaning of life is real. The pain is deep. The sorrow at times can be overwhelming. O Lord my cup is running over. I'm the eldest. No question, I have to stay. Mom's girls have to make the final arrangements together. We had to find mom something to be buried in. We had to write the obituary. We had to notify her friends. We had to have everything done as quickly as possible. I made the appointment with the funeral home. We were scheduled to make arrangements the next day. Lord, this is really happening?

Lord I can't be two places at once! I need a little help down here. My daughter is counting on me. I need to make the trip to South Carolina. I have to call and talk with Nakisha and Bobby. I have to break the news about

Granny. I have to rework the travel plans. Lord its' too much!

On The Road Again Heading East

Everything was complete. I had done all that could be done for mom. I stopped by the funeral home. I dropped off her suit. The obituary for the printer was hand delivered. The pictures for the DVD were completed in the proper order. Mom would have a video played at her viewing and at her services. I was headed out, finally South Carolina bound. On any normal road trip I often played hours of music to soothe my soul. It helped me to focus on the road while in prayer and meditation. I couldn't concentrate this time. The music was on but I couldn't absorb it. It became the symphony of my tears. So for ten hours I wept. The music helped me to purge the sorrows of my heart.

By the time I got to Nashville, I had only stopped for restroom breaks. I had nibbled on salty chips to settle my stomach. My very dear sister-friend lived south of Nashville about 20 minutes in Franklin, Tennessee. I had called ahead. I let her know I would need a place to crash for a few hours' sleep.

Delores was a former church member who had moved away many years ago. She was my sister in Christ. She was my confidante as well. She opened her home to me. She welcomed me in as she always did. She had no idea what news I was going to share.

I let Delores coerce me into a few bites of some food. I was exhausted. With mixed emotions I broke the news to her about Mom. She hugged me and was my soft place to land. I asked her to let me sleep about four hours. Then I would get back on the road. Lord, now I lay me down to sleep I pray dear lord my soul, my soul needs sleep. Help me Lord.

Startled I awoke to discover it was six hours later than I planned to resume my trip. As I tried to fuss at Delores for letting me over sleep, she just smiled. As I tried to fuss some more she said softly, "Debra, I don't care what you said. You needed sleep. And I'm not sorry about it either."

I saw that mischievous twinkle in her eyes. You can't get mad when you hear the voice of reason. I just love how she mothered on me. It was just what I needed. I hugged her. I thanked her. I told her how much I loved her. As I filled up the car at a nearby gas station, I began to hear the birds chirping as the sun started to rise. I was back on the road, just me and God. I found my prayer language. I began to sing.

Peace Be Still

For the rest of the trip, I sang and I prayed. By the time I arrived at the parsonage in Rock Hill I had a genuine peace. Kisha and Bobby helped me bring my stuff in. Kisha had heard most of the story by now from Kelli. I just filled in the blanks. They both seemed worried about how I was doing. For the first time in days, I assured them I was okay. My daughter seemed at peace. Her Mom had arrived safely.

Everyone who makes up proverbs will say of you,
'Like mother, like daughter.'
Ezekiel 16:44

We talked. We packed. We loaded the truck. We cleaned the house in preparation for the new family. A professional cleaning crew was coming to complete the job on Monday. Life was happening. I was keeping busy.

This was Kisha and Bobby's first pastoral charge since they left seminary. They had done well. They had grown the membership. They were great with the youth. I had come to visit several times. I had grown to love the church. I had grown to love the people too.

The kids drafted me into service at their church. I served in many areas; teaching, women's ministry, cooking, cleaning and everything in between. I was there for the Hurricane Katrina disaster relief effort. They serviced many relocated families. On one trip I was the only cook for 200 people at a breakfast. I had never handled a commercial kitchen by myself before. I was baptized by fire. I was going to miss this church. This church was part of my story.

Saying Goodbye Is Always Hard

Then Jesus said, "Come to me, all of you who are weary
and carry heavy burdens, and I will give you rest.
Take my yoke upon you. Let me teach you, because I
am humble and gentle at heart,
and you will find rest for your souls.
For my yoke is easy to bear, and the burden
I give you is light."
Matthew 11:28-30

Farewell Sunday had finally arrived. I managed the babies. The reception was beautiful, not a dry eye in the house. I was so glad I had become a part of such a beautiful church relationship. We were on the road by 2 pm. The return trip was long for two toddlers. We stopped in Jackson, Tennessee to rest overnight with the kids. They were having an awful time and were pretty cranky. Being Nana for a few days helped to refill my soul. It took my mind off what lay ahead, Mom's funeral.

The next morning began with renewed stress. We were late getting started. We had a deadline to make. We had to be in Oklahoma City by 6 PM. My church was bringing dinner to my home. It was the night before saying good-bye to Mom. I had to get home. The truck could not go very fast. At one point I had to apologize to Kisha but we needed to speed up. I stopped so that she could let Bobby know we would be going on ahead. He understood and agreed to drive alone.

Once Bobby reached Oklahoma, he would go north to Sapulpa. He would unload the truck. Bobby would meet us in the morning in Oklahoma City well before the service. We kept West on I-40 just above the speed limit to make up time. God already made preparation for just such a time as this. When Bobby arrived in Sapulpa, the men of the new church were waiting. They unloaded the truck in record time. The new church had already been informed of the family tragedy.

Kisha, the babies and I arrived at my home in Oklahoma City at 6:30 PM. My church was already there. The food was hot and ready to eat. We had our devotion.

For the net hour I let my church minister to me and my family. Kelli and my sisters had arranged for others to come during the same time. People came and went dropping off more food. We visited and greeted all the guests as a family. When everyone left we all crashed. What a day!

Honoring Mom

The next day we celebrated the life of my mother. The choir sang all of Mom's favorite hymns. Songs that told her story, her life journey. Her life was the story of a soldier's journey. Mom along with her first husband, my stepdad, raised me. Along came my two sisters, his two girls. He was in the Air Force for the first twelve years of our lives. I learned a lot from Mom about how to survive. How to make decisions on the fly.

The service was an awesome testimony to the life she had. She was a soldier's wife and a soldier for God. It reminded me just how lovingly God had cared for her. In spite of her health, she was faithful to her church. She was a true soldier in every sense of the word. During the service

I remembered Mom was the one who took me to my first simultaneous Baptist revival service. I was Christian Methodist and twelve. What did I know?

Mom was my most loyal bible student. When I taught the scriptures she adored my teachings. She was so proud of my anointing in the word. This classy sassy lady was no more. Her pastor said, "You did not have to wonder what Sister Jenkins thought. She always let you know! The whole church laughed through their tears.

At the dinner, I looked around the room. I realized I personally knew all of her lifelong friends. I marveled at the thought of how special that was. How they watched me grow up. How they supported me. How they loved her. It really does take a village to raise a child. I was humbled to be her daughter.

I thanked God for the many years we sang in the choir together. How she worked side by side with all of her girls in the church. I thanked God for the legacy she gave me as a daughter in Christ. I could hear her voice singing, "Precious Memories, how they linger, how they ever flood my soul." Thank you God for my mother, a second generation strong woman of God.

What memories about your loved one gives you peace? Are there special songs they sang or you liked to hear that invoke smiles and laughter about your loved one. What makes the music so special and soothing. What image about your loved one do you hold dear? I experience healing every time I tell a story from my Mom's point of view. I start by saying, "If Mom were hear she would say _____." How you complete the sentence about your loved one?

Reflections

1. What gives you hope?

2. What gives you strength?

3. What gives you comfort?

4. What gives you meaning to life?

5. What gives you peace?

6. What makes you feel loved?

7. What makes you feel connected?

8. What is preventing you from doing all the things you've listed here?

9. How can you change this so that you can answer each question and feel good about the answers?

CHAPTER FOUR – HANGING BY A THREAD

In the midst of all this hurt life kept happening. I had to make sure Devin was doing well. He was still fragile. Things for Devin and I had been stressful. My health had deteriorated. It was 2003. I had a lumbar fusion surgery on my lower back. I had just come home from the hospital.

Devin's health had nose-dived as well. Devin went into renal failure. He was in ICU for about 10 days. The ramifications of his declining health took a toll on both his marriages. His first marriage ended three months after the birth of his son. Now his second marriage was ending. When he was released from the hospital, Devin moved in with me. We were both bedridden and needing assistance. My family and lifelong friends came to the rescue.

Devin went to dialysis three times per week. Every Monday, Wednesday and Friday at 5 AM sharp. It was our routine to get Devin up and moving on time. Medi-ride transported him back and forth most days. I was not well enough to drive. My Aunt Hallie, Mom's baby sister, took

Devin to dialysis when he could not reserve a ride or missed his ride.

Devin appeared to be drained a lot when he got home. He made bad decisions about his health. He would come home after his treatments and go to sleep without eating. His blood sugar would drop during his nap. He would go into seizures or worse while he slept. EMT's were coming to the house every day or every other day. This went on from 2003 to 2006. It was mind boggling now that I remember.

Worn Torn and Poured Out

After mom died, being in charge of Devin's health was getting to be too much. I needed time to grieve my mother. Devin needed to finally take responsibility for his own health. His escalating diabetic episodes were happening way too often. I was stretched beyond all human limits. I just couldn't keep this pace going. How dare he assume it was my job to take care of him? He was a grown man! I knew deep down he could not control the things happening inside his body. But I was becoming bitter and resentful. Is there such a thing as PTSD for caregivers? Lord help me!

It was around that time we were told Devin had heart disease. When his heart would stop it would be without warning. He was told he would feel no pain. The doctor called it "the silent killer". Devin did not take the news well. I was devastated. What more can happen Lord? This was out of his control. What about everything else? The things happening to his body I could understand. There was a medical reason. It was the things Devin could do and wouldn't that made me mad. Lord forgive me. I was trying hard to contain my primal scream. My cup is running over Lord.

Sometimes Devin would fuzz out while awake. He would try to do the last thing he remembered. One day the neighbor found him wandering around the back yard. Thank God the neighbor was a nurse on his day off.

One day Devin's friend came by to pick him up. He didn't answer the door. His friend called Kelli. Kelli called 911. The fire department used a ram to force the front door in. They found him unconscious inside. I called my friend to come over and board up the front door from the inside.

The very next day the fire department got a call from Devin on his cell phone. He was inside the house. He was losing consciousness. He was not able to come open the door. The firemen forced open the side garage door. Now I had to have both doors repaired. There are no words, Lord, so let me hold my peace.

Devin had turned over tables, chairs, pulled down curtains, broken lamps, broken furniture and everything in his path while in his semi-conscious state. I was constantly trying to get the blood out of the carpet. Blood stains were in all the places where EMT's had performed lifesaving procedures or had to give IV's to bring Devin back. Every day was getting to be too much. I resented his selfish attitude. I needed more grace. Help me Holy Spirit!

I'm Not Superwoman

I was being pushed to my limit. Devin wouldn't quit driving. I never knew when he would pass out at the wheel while driving. He had done this before. He had a medical emergency while driving in the year 2000. That was the day I was moving into this new home.

I got a call that Devin passed out at the wheel. His son and three step kids were in the car. He went into a diabetic coma while driving. Devin an SUV head on. The engine of his car ended up in his lap. Devin had an eight hour surgery to put a steel rod in his leg from the hip socket to the ankle. All the kids were injured. Devin II had a separated collar bone. Dominic had an almost severed ear from the seat beat. JaQue had bruised kidneys. Ashlee had a head injury. God healed them all. None of us could possibly keep going on like that. We all deserved better.

Here We Go Again

Both mothers had been warned to never let Devin drive the kids around in his car. Every friend was told to stop riding in the car when Devin was driving as well. I was concerned about everyone's safety. His doctor would not take his license away. I tried to reason with him to but no avail.

I was home one Sunday after church. It was early July, 2006. It was literally a couple of weeks after mom's funeral. I got a call from Devin's second ex-wife. Devin had left church driving home alone. He was acting erratic. She stated his car was weaving. She thought he was in trouble. She followed him in her car. She could tell he was losing consciousness but he was still driving north on a busy street. She was hysterical. I panicked.

Devin would soon be coming to a major intersection. My fear was if he was not fully conscious he would hit someone. He could injure someone else. He could possibly himself. By the grace of God, he negotiated the turn. He was coming down the major street that was directly parallel to the street we lived on. I prayed the whole time like never before.

Kelli got in her car and drove to the end of the street. She waited at the intersection. I called 911. The 911 Operator stated they had multiple calls about the incident and officers were in route. The street was a four lane divided road with two lanes each way. Kelli called me on her cell minutes later. "Mom he's weaving from one side of the road to the other across all four lanes. Cars are avoiding him. His head is fully back on the headrest. He drove right past me." Before I could think what to do next, we both heard the crash. It was loud and horrific sounding. My heart stopped beating. I couldn't breathe. I slid down to the floor and just cried. Devin was less than two blocks from home. The crash happened right in front of the fire station. The fire station was empty. The fire crew was out on another emergency run. Kelli raced to the scene. EMT's met her there.

Devin had hit a car broadside. The other driver was a 90 year old woman. The air bags of both cars deployed. The Lady appeared to have only scratches. That wasn't the point. She had a right to go wherever she wanted safely. Devin didn't care and I was at the end of my rope. The woman was transported to the hospital as a precaution to be checked out. Devin was unconscious and transported as well. Both cars were total losses.

How Long God Can This Go On?

I am sick at heart. How long,

O LORD, until you restore me? Psalm 6:3

As Kelli and I waited in the ER, I became despondent. Lord, I can't take much more of this. Please help me. I was upset over another wave of never ending crisis. I worried that the elderly lady was ok. I was so angry at Devin for not listening. I was fed up with all of the drama. I knew this was by no means the end. The woman was released with facial scratches. Thank God for his mercy. What a miracle it wasn't worse. Hear my prayer O God!

Devin was revived. He was banged and bruised but he recovered. I was over the top with anger. Lord help me not say anything I might have to repent from later? When Devin saw me, He could not even look me in the eye. He knew he should not be driving. He was being so stubborn and strong willed. He seemed to be trying to squeeze a lifetime of living all right now. What upset me was he didn't count the cost of such selfish motives. When he was released from the hospital I took him home, my home.

Later that night when I tried to talk with him, Devin began raging. DeCarla came over and we just let him vent. He was hurt. He was scared. He was worried about his health deteriorating. I was worried. It was in God's hands. My Lord!

I Turn Him Over to You Lord

It was now an afternoon in late July 2006. I had to come out of retirement to work a temporary job with an Insurance agency. I was trying to pay for all the damage around my home. Kelli called. Devin was driving again. No surprise, He had another medical emergency.

Devin had taken his son and a friend's son to little league football practice. He was one of the coaches that founded the team. Devin refused to give up on the team. My first thought; have these mom's lost their minds? To their credit I later found out they didn't know.

The story went as they were leaving practice Devin passed out at the wheel. Little Devin got into the front seat. He sat on his dad's lap. Somehow that 11 year old managed to apply the brakes. He guided the car to a complete stop on the side of the road. Little Devin's friend in the back seat called both their Mom's. Both families made it to the scene before first responders. Both families picked up the boys and took them home. Little Devin's mom stayed with my son Devin. She called 911 from her cell phone. She waited for EMT's to arrive. God was with him still. I was done.

Oh Lord, you know. I can't keep doing this. I won't keep this up. Enough is enough. I had to believe that God was going to work this out. I need you right now Lord. My cup is overflowing. This weight is too heavy. I was so mad; way past angry. Lord don't let me say anything this time. I might just have to repent for something. And it might not be pretty.

Oh, how I longed for the peaceful sound of music. I needed a song, something to take my mind away from all my troubles. I could not comprehend the emptiness of my soul. I gave and gave, O Lord, I don't know how long I can hang in there. Jesus!

Reflections

1. What are your faith traditions when things get too hard?
2. Is there a special place you like to go?
3. Is there something that you do that settles your spirit and allows you to regain your peace?
4. Self-care is important. Life is about balance. Are you consciously eating, sleeping and getting enough rest?
5. Do you have a soft place to land? A person you can call or go visit that makes you feel better?
6. Have you tried journaling your thoughts? If not would you consider doing it?
7. Have you tried deep breathing exercises?
8. Have you considered laugh therapy?
9. Have you considered just letting the scream come out? Let it go, let it happen.

CHAPTER FIVE –
THE FACE OF WRONG CHOICES

It was now August 6th, 2006. I was working it out, just God and me. I had finally finished all the paperwork associated with someone dying. I had taken care of everybody that needed caring for. I was just now realizing a new normal. My mother was gone. I did not have the time to grieve.

There was drama everywhere. There was too much going on. Things were in a constant state of confusion. Mom had two sisters left. Helen was the oldest, Hallie was the youngest. Both Aunts were in poor health. We were all struggling to make it. I had to make myself available for the Aunties. They needed me. I was the next person in line. I can do this. I'm doing this. And then I got that call.

"Hello." It was about 8:00 P.M. when a sobbing voice said, "Cousin Debra, you've got to come, come now! Helen told me to call you. We just found Traci dead!" I know I didn't hear her correctly. "Traci?" she responded, "Yes, Traci. She was up a few hours ago. She cooked dinner for her grandkids. She went to lie down. We can't wake her. Helen says she's gone." I told her I was on the way. I hung up. Traci was Aunt Helen's only daughter. I was afraid this would send Helen's health into a downward spiral. Alright Lord, my cup is running over!

I went to tell my daughter Kelli I was headed to Helen's house. She jumped up and said, "You are not going to the Eastside of town at night by yourself." I said, "I have to. Helen needs me." I headed out the door. I knew she was calling in re-enforcements but I had to go.

When I pulled up to the house it was 9:00 PM. There was a crowd of about 100 people standing on the opposite side of the street. It looked like broad daylight. There was a large crowd in the front yard. The OKC Police were on site. They were there to protect the scene. I just walked through the crowd in the yard and into the house. This is the house I grew up in. The house my Grandmama built.

Not The House That Alice Built

Who are all these folk? I don't know these people. The only person I needed to see was my Aunt. Inside the door, I waded through each person; comforting cousin Traci's daughter, hugging Traci's son. I kissed Traci's grandbabies. Her grandbabies were crying, each and every one. I went past the first bedroom with the officer standing guard outside the door.

I went into the second bedroom. I found my Aunt. I sat down next to Aunt Helen on her bed. I saw tears running down her face. She was crying but I heard no sound. I heard no music. What I heard was the clock ticking off time. In the distance I could hear muffled sobbing but still no music. I reached out. I held Helen's hand. We both just waited, together. We waited for the Medical Examiner to arrive.

It was Debra, Denise, Dawn and Traci in that order. We all grew up in Grandmama Alice's frame house. We ate the same food. Lived by the same rules. We all grew up and graduated high school. It was at that point our paths took different turns. Traci turned to the streets. Traci became addicted to cocaine. Traci had a son. Traci didn't care to name him. So I came up with his name, Andre Tyrell. Traci had a daughter that she decided she would name this child Angela.

Traci decided there was money to be made in selling drugs. So, naturally she sold drugs. She ran the third largest drug house in the City. Traci lived on the edge. She introduced her two brothers, Gregory and Darryl to the drug life. Everything comes to an end. The police raided her drug home and Traci was busted. She went to prison for most of her adult life. Her brothers also went to prison. Helen was alone to raise Traci's two kids. She raised Gregory's son, Gregory Jr. but we called him Baby Greg. Life was hard for Helen. I did all I could to make their lives as normal as possible. There was no beauty in the drug life. It was hard, dark, and merciless.

The kids needed stability. I stepped in to help. When my kids went to church, I took Andre, Angela and Baby Greg. When my kids went skating, on a picnic, Easter Egg Hunt, Halloween, Carnivals, Zoo, or anywhere I took

Andre, Angela and Baby Greg. Life was hard and it wasn't fair. I had to be the disciplinarian for kids not of my body. They needed structure. I became the game changer in their lives. I was determined to keep the innocents from sharing a jail cell with their parents.

Traci was in and out prison. She spent more time in than out. She had been released from prison in April, 2006. Here it was August and life for Traci was over. She died of a heart attack in her sleep. No one was ready to lose her. Not her kids, not her grandkids and certainly not her mother.

Love and Support

While I waited with Helen in the bedroom, the Family Calvary had arrived. It was good to see those I loved. My family who I trusted had my back. After the ME took the body away we sat down to a family meeting. Of course there was no money. The only insurance policy had lapsed. We had to raise the money. The choice of a funeral or cremation all depended on what the family came up with.

Our family had never had a cremation. We didn't believe in it. Everyone was together in the family cemetery. We were taught to stay together. Our tradition was to care for our loved ones even to the grave. The weight of that thought I left on her two adult kids to figure out. I gave them a deadline to come up with the money. I was numb. I was tired of being the only one capable of making the hard choices. It was time Traci's family stepped up.

My side of the family raised part of the money. Traci's kids came up with the rest. I scheduled the funeral at one of our sister churches to hold the large crowd we expected. Traci had a reputation of being large and in charge. That meant prison folk, street folk and family would co-mingle to pay our last respects. I went and paid for the arrangements with the money raised. My sister Dawn paid for the family spray. My church paid for the funeral programs. We made the best of a bad situation.

One evening two days before the funeral I went by to check on my Aunt. She was so tired from grieving she had not been resting. She fell asleep and fell out of the bed. She was 80 years old. There were too many street folk in the house making noise and disrespecting her. There was no time for me to grieve. I needed to keep moving. I had no rhythm other than the beat of my own heart, hurrying to get things done.

I had to constantly go by the house. I checked on Aunt Helen. I ran off the less desirable folk. I didn't plan on backing away from the challenge. I didn't mind laying holy hands on folk to lift them up and out of my aunt's home. It was marital law around the old homestead. The word was out. There was a new sheriff in town by the name of Debra. I was in a taking no prisons kind of mood. They didn't know who I was or how I was related but the word was out. No drinking, no drugging and no mess allowed. I was over all of it. Thank you God for strength of this never ending storm.

At one point I had to get real strict with the prison Muslims. They wanted to take over the final arrangements. Aunt Helen would always tell them you have to clear that with Debra. Traci became Muslim in prison for protection to survive. It didn't matter the reason. We were raised as Christians. We lived as Christians. We weren't having it.

Everything was done decent and in order. In the end Traci had a beautiful service. Aunt Helen was well pleased. Andre and Angela were satisfied. I did what I had to do for the family. We buried our dead. The day after the service I realized I was running on way past empty. I was all poured out. Jesus I need you. I need you Lord right now!

I pray that God, the source of hope,
will fill you completely with joy and
peace because you trust in him.
Then you will overflow with confident hope
through the power of the Holy Spirit.
Romans 15:13

Reflections

1. Did you have unfinished business with the person you are grieving for?

2. Can you name the feelings holding you back?

3. Are you ready to deal with your issues at this time in your life?

4. If not what do you need to work on to be ready?

5. How does holding on to these issues affect how you view your family and friends?

6. How have your beliefs influenced your behavior and mood during this time?

7. What role might your belief system play in resolving your issues?

8. Have you considered ways to let go of the unfinished business?

CHAPTER SIX – THE REAL DEAL

Mom's gone, check. I'm still pinching myself about Traci's death. Check, check. And now my son is not breathing. This can't be real. I can't see Devin's face. I need to see his face. Always before when he was unconscious his face would be twisted. The struggle of fighting his way back would be on his face. I could not see his face. His face was turned to the wall. Lord please let me see his face. Devin is dead. It is best to leave him alone until the official word was given to move him.

Firemen To The Rescue

We lived just around the corner from the Fire Station No. 15. I could hear the sirens headed our way. As they often do when they turned down our street they would turn the sirens off. They did this to avoid disturbing the neighbors. I went to leave the door open. All they had to do was walk in. I didn't think about safety. Death had already entered in my home past the door and the locks. Darkness traveled with death and delivered my grief. I shivered but not from the cool morning air.

The firemen knew the way to Devin's house. This was a regular run for the firemen. This time the run would end differently. It took a few minutes but fire rescue arrived. The Fire Chief entered the door first. He stated, "It's Devin right." I nodded yes. "Is he in his room?" I nodded yes again. With the next question the Chief stopped in his tracks, turned and looked directly at me, "Is he gone?" I nodded yes one more time. Then Chief said, "Let me go check" as he disappeared into Devin's room. He wasn't gone long but everything now moved in slow motion.

As I think about it now, it's really rare that everyone at the fire station knew the direction to Devin's house. The firemen knew where Devin's room was located. The firemen could recite all of Devin's medical information verbatim to EMT's when they arrived. I never had to say a word. Too many visits, too many episodes trying to keep Devin alive. I appreciated their care and concern. None of this was normal. Right now the EMT's were my only lifeline.

When the Chief returned as expected he said, "I'm so sorry. Yes, he's gone. I would say since about 2 am." I became keenly aware by that time all twelve members of OKC's finest firemen stood in my living room. The fireman stood with heads down, holding their helmets. I thanked them. They mounted up. There was nothing left to do. As they got back on the truck, the OKC Police Officer came in next. I showed her to Devin's door. She stood watch. As she did she offered her condolences as well.

A New Reality

I went in search of Kelli. I found her on the floor in my bedroom sobbing. Her big brother, her protector was gone. Little did I know in the short time she was in my room she had called the Family Calvary once again. The front door opened and my Sister Dawn & her husband Ron arrived first. She sat with me as I began to make notification calls. His kids needed to know their Dad had died. I called Devin's first ex-wife, little Devin's mom. It did not go well. It did not go well at all. Dawn said, "Let's not call anyone else just yet." I had no problem complying with that request. I was not up to the task. At least not yet.

Roland and DeCarla burst through the door. DeCarla just realizing that something wasn't right fell on her knees with her head in my lap. "Did he die! Is Devin gone?" she asked. Softly I whispered yes, Devin is gone. She cried hysterical now, "I'm sorry." I just patted her head in my lap as she cried. I said, "it's going to be okay." I nodded hello at DeCarla's husband Roland. By the grace of God it had to be Okay. I just wasn't clear on how God would make it happen.

I looked up to see the Police Officer crying softly as well. I nodded again. Ron got her some tissues. Kelli came out of the bedroom. I explained that the call to little Devin's house did not go well. Alyssa had spent the night here with her daddy. Devin fed her cookies until 10 pm. The last thing I did was fuss Devin out about feeding the baby cookies. If I had known this would be the last time we would talk, I would have said something different. I would have said Devin I love you. I would have said so much more. All I remember saying was "Son are you feeling okay?" I can see him smiling. I know in my heart right now that he is.

I do remember reminding Alyssa she was forbidden to sleep with her dad. She loved her daddy. She always wanted to sleep with him. Sometimes she would sneak into bed with him when I fell asleep. Thank God last night she complied. I shudder to think how this would have turned out if she had been in bed with her dad when he died.

I asked Kelli to call Alyssa's mom. She was Devin's second ex-wife. Alyssa now aged 5 years old was asleep in her Aunt Kelli's room. God had miraculously kept that baby sleep through all the commotion. I needed her mom to come get her before the house filled up with mourners. To her Mom's credit she came right away. She met Kelli at the open garage door and took Devin's sweet baby girl Alyssa home.

Death Doesn't Discriminate

Kelli called the funeral home that our family used. They were personal friends and former church members. Our kids grew up at church together. They were sending someone. Kelli then called her sister's home. She reached Bobby on the phone. The call was short, quick and to the point. It didn't take long.

Kisha called right back. I answered the phone. She was out of breath. I knew then for sure Kelli had called her. "Mom, we're on our way. It will take us about one and a half hours to get there from Sapulpa. I promise we are headed out as fast as we can." I knew instinctively something had been lost in the translation. Reality had not yet set in. I answered slowly, "There's no rush Kisha. Be safe. Take your time. I'll see you when you get here." Kisha was quiet for a few seconds, "Oh" pause, "Oh my". That's when I realized she had not fully heard what she had been told earlier. "Devin's gone so there's no reason to rush. Take your time Kisha." Lord, Lord, I prayed!

The door opened. In came Kelli's Pastor and his wife. They looked as if they were just going to church, fully dressed, not a hair out of place at 6 AM. I was truly impressed. We had prayer. At times like these you can never have too much prayer. Right now I needed to hear angels up above my head. Cover me Lord. This was just the beginning.

The next time the door opened it was Missy, Kelli's friend since grade school. She was crying. I had to hug and console her first. I asked her to please go in and comfort Kelli right now. She had done enough today. She needs someone just for her. Missy agreed to help.

In came Little Devin, his mother, grandmother and two brothers in tow. They all had the deer in headlights look. They were shocked and devastated. I found out later Devin had talked on the phone to his son first and then his ex-wife now his fiancé until midnight. Little Devin was beyond grief. He could not comprehend the loss of his father. He would not leave my side. Lord thank you his last words were to his son.

My extended family came to my aid. The physician called and talked to me about what transpired. I answered all his questions. The coroner had spoken with the physician. Due to Devin's extensive medical history with diabetes, renal failure and heart disease, the coroner released the body. The Police Officer left. The funeral home sent one elderly gentleman by himself to pick Devin up. My two brothers in laws, Ron and Roland assisted the worker to get Devin out of the house. He was loaded into the hearse. The hearse drove away. Finally Devin's room was empty. The house was no longer a safe refuge. Death resided in to my home. If music had a sound right now it would be a low guttural moan.

Before I could ask everyone started cleaning, answering the phone, cooking and whatever they thought needed doing. I was relieved. I just sat down and contemplated my life without my son. For me there was no music. I heard music. It was noise, just background noise. I kept asking Roland and Ron what Devin's face looked like. Was his face twisted? For some reason they couldn't or wouldn't say. Everyone was trying to protect me. What I needed was the truth, no matter how hard or unkind. I was waiting on someone to hear what I needed to get through this. Lord is anyone willing to listen to me? Father, can you hear me?

As the night turned to morning I remembered Elijah, afraid, hovering in the bowels of his cave. Sometimes in the stillness, in the quiet, God's soft voice is all the music we need.

Reflections

1. Do you believe in the power of prayer?

2. When do you like to pray?

3. Do you go into a secret room, just you and God?

4. How has prayer worked in your life?

5. Have your prayers been answered?

6. Do you keep a prayer journal?

7. Do you pray for others?

8. If it's been a while would you consider praying now?

CHAPTER SEVEN - IT'S ABOUT FORGIVENESS

I look up to the mountains—

does my help come from there?

My help comes from the LORD,

who made heaven and earth!

He will not let you stumble;

the one who watches over you will not slumber.

Indeed, he who watches over Israel

never slumbers or sleeps.

The LORD himself watches over you!

The LORD stands beside you as your protective shade.

The sun will not harm you by day,

nor the moon at night.

The LORD keeps you from all harm

and watches over your life.

The LORD keeps watch over you as you come and go,

both now and forever. Psalms 121:1-8

Doing What Needs To Be Done

I had to make the arrangements. This was to be a
celebration to God for the extra years he blessed Devin to

be here. I had not forgotten all the physicians that didn't think Devin would make it this far. One doctor said he would never live to see age 16. God knew better. I planned a Home Going service for just that reason. I made a mental note to look for God at work in every detail. God was in the planning and the preparation. We were going to come together as one united family in our loss.

I found Devin's favorite purple suit. Kisha had it cleaned. The girls and I looked for his trademark big faced watch and silver chain necklace. We found the watch but no chain necklace. Together we would go as a family to take care of our loved one. Kisha, Kelli and I would take care of Devin one last time.

Death affects everyone. It does not discriminate in how it exerts its painful control. The funeral director's son called to say he just realized our deceased was Devin, his friend. They grew up at church together. Sometimes partners in crime. It was Devin and he just couldn't prepare him personally. I let him know it was alright. Just pick someone he trusted to take care of him. Lord take care of the funeral director, he needs you too.

When I arrived the Owner of the funeral home and my former church member attended to me himself. I appreciated the dignity, care and concern he showed toward me. He included small upgrades that were both precious and memorable for me as a mom. The silver casket would go nice with the suit. The flowers in purple and white. Devin's name was to be embroidered on the inside lining in purple. Purple was Devin's favorite color. The love of purple was something we both shared. The details were perfect. The insurance policy was exactly enough to cover the entire service. God was working things out.

God At Work

When everything was complete the family went to view. To our surprise Devin had on his jewelry. I did ask the directors where they found the jewelry. I was told Devin had it on. They had it polished. He looked asleep. He had a smile on his face. That was what I was waiting for. That's what I needed to see. If they had just told me I would not have stressed out over it. God was still working.

Thank God for obedience. God told me to write Devin's obituary last year. When I heard that message I immediately fell prostate on my bedroom floor. I cried or rather whaled for a reprieve. I prayed and asked God to relent. When I did not get an answer, I got up and tearfully wrote the obituary.

I am so glad I did as I was told. My mind was not fully capable of thinking of all the things I needed to remember. It was all there, written down. I needed only to fill in the dates and any updates on names that I did not have correctly. At that moment again I realized God was working in the details. He was the music in the background of my life. God was perfection in the midst of my chaos.

I did ask God to give me strength to write a poem. A special memorial from a mother's heart to her son. This is what God gave me to say:

Reflections of a Mothers Love to a Son

Devin T. Hamilton

April 25, 1973 to August 21, 2006

I counted fingers and toes, they were all there
I found only fuzz that should have been hair
With love and trust you looked at my face
So young and unsure what I needed was grace
Your tiny hands held securely to mine
That bond we repeated many times.

Gone was the baby, you stood so tall
My little man, you learned how to fall
To land on your feet when the going was rough
Oh how stubborn, so proud, and so tough
As you learned of life with wonder and joy
I was so proud you were my little boy.

Time passed quickly, memories grew
Gone was the toddler I once knew.
You grew up to be a Godly man
One who reached up to hold God's hand.

No matter what trials, what aches or pain
You had a Savior and called on his name.
He lifted you up in the palm of his hand
Far beyond my hopes and all of my plans
Your feet are now planted in his Garden of Care
We will see you again when we get there.
Love Mama ©2006 Debra Lynn Spears

It took fifteen minutes, a lot of tears and tissue to get to the end. I knew it was exactly what I wanted for the program. I ordered 450 programs. We ran out. Thank you Holy Spirit for the anointing to do what must be done for my son.

Reconciliation

There also were some things that weren't surprises after all. Devin's bio dad and I were both too young. He could not accept the responsibilities of parenthood. I had no other options. On the day we were to be married we both backed out. It was a mutual decision. We were good friends. But we were not in love. We would have married for all the wrong reasons.

It was two months before the baby was due. When the decision was made to break up I cried. I cried about being a future single parent. I didn't cry about the breakup. Devin met his dad officially when he turned 18. He did everything he could to learn about his bio family. Now Devin is gone. Bio dad never came over to the house to offer condolences. He never contacted me about the funeral arrangements. He, his wife and three sons were Jehovah's Witness. I wasn't sure they would enter the church. Entering the church was against their doctrine. Surprisingly they did come into the church. Bio dad however showed up to the service drunk. No surprises there.

I met the man who would help raise my son. Devin was two months old at the time. My girlfriend got married. She and her new husband were moving into their first apartment. I went over to help them. Her new husband had invited his friend over to help as well. The newlyweds introduced us. We double dated. Through some match making on their part we got together. Seven months later we were married.

Our marriage lasted for 13 years. Our marriage produced my two beautiful daughters before it failed. You would expect stepdad to come immediately when he got the news Devin was gone. He was the only dad Devin knew. He had raised Devin his whole life. That's what I expected. Devin's stepdad did not come over until he was sure all the funeral arrangements had been made. He checked with the girls to make sure I still had the insurance policy I purchased all those years ago. I was angry and felt betrayed. Did our relationship come down to money? Out of the abundance of the heart the mouth speaks.

When stepdad finally came to the house, he stated he didn't understand why his family was coming from out of town for the funeral. Kelli told him, "Dad to the rest of the world your son died". He had no clue. When he viewed the body, I was told he took it extremely hard. He told Kisha, "Some of us have regrets". Kisha told him, "Dad, some of us don't."

Stepdad disconnected from Devin when the divorce happened for some reason. He became distant in his attitude as the nurturing father for Devin. Evidently he still had issues and didn't want to financially support him. His family never knew and I wasn't going to tell them. They would have to just figure it out on their own. I didn't have time to deal with it. I was so proud of both my girls. They stood with me. We were united, together. The girls hung in there even though things were extremely hard for us to deal with. We shared a family grief song, the brokenness of our hearts.

I had to let the negative feelings go. The thought of the pettiness was too taxing to worry about right now. Who deals with such things at a time like this? Later stepdad did end up paying the balance due on the headstone the girls and I ordered. When he paid the balance he made certain to remind me; if bio dad ever gave me any money he wanted a refund on his money. All I could say was wow! I didn't see that one coming!

I'm not shaming, throwing blame or guilt anywhere. It is what it is. In spite of all the material issues my son was going to be taken care of. God began to impress on me Devin's home going service would be anointed. Devin's life and death would break the chains of unforgiveness, anger, betrayal, heartache and pain people were carrying around even to this day. I trusted that word of knowledge. I needed to see something good come out of something so painful.

The Way It Should Be

Even through moments of grief, I could see God working it all out. The funeral procession was to start at my home. The home where Devin died. I pulled both ex-wives aside together. I told them I loved them both. I told them today was my day. I had to say good-bye to my son. I let them know they were in charge of their own kids today. Nana wasn't available. Today, I was a mother, grieving for her son. I did not have the strength to deal with negative emotions. To my amazement, immediately after "the talk", the mothers' hugged each other. I was so stunned I had to sit down. I could not talk, there were no words for the power of love I had just witnessed. I cried tears of joy. Finally, thank you Lord.

God began to show me he had me surrounded with love. His anointing was tangible. I could see it everywhere.

The County Sheriff and his hand-picked crew lead the processional to the church. The sheriff was a family friend. His dad grew up next door to my mother's family. Our grandparents were friends. God's love runs deep.

I saw firsthand nothing is too hard for God to work out. As we pulled into the church both the maternal and paternal sides of my family were in the processional. There were two huge family groups assembled in front of the church. I recognized one group as Devin's bio family. The other group was my ex- husband's family. The family that loved and helped to raise Devin as their own without question.

I began to praise God. It was happening. Devin's death was the one event that could put broken family relationships back together. All negative things were put under Jesus feet with this one solitary life. Jesus was present. As we proceeded into the church the choir did as instructed. The choir sang songs of praise and celebration to God the minute we stepped into the sanctuary. That set the tone for the entire service.

I let stepdad as head of the family walk in first with our daughters. It didn't matter what order we entered. A united family, today that was what we were, good, bad or ugly. This was Devin's day. This was his church. The church that loved him.

Some church members had no idea they were related to Devin until they read the obituary. Some of his friends were also his family. Testimonies were shared about Devin's last weekend. From Friday to Sunday night Devin had personally talked to a large majority of the mourners. My how that young man got around. I thanked God for their stories it gave me courage and lifted my heart.

Little Devin's football team was there in full uniform. Those 11 year olds handmade sympathy cards for him about his dad. They wore black arm bands for the occasion. After service they huddled up surrounding Little Devin with love in the innocent way only kids can. I was so proud, I cried. Thank you God.

As the songs were sung I began to feel my heart song

coming forth. I began to worship. I began to pray. Little Devin had a nose bleed and had to be attended to. The mothers worked together to care for the kids. Baby Alyssa kept saying that's my dad all during the service. The church would cry every time she did. None of it took away from my worship. I kept singing, "Praise is what I do, even when I'm going through".

I began to heal. The Eulogy was perfect. Devin had 33 years to live his life. He lived it to the fullest. For a guy that came into the world at 33 weeks and left the world at 33 years, he did great. No one is perfect. I released the weight of his illness. I realized I was still holding tight to it. I loved my son. Down here, Devin showed love every chance he got. He was human. He made some bad decisions and bad choices. But he lived well. He visited often. He loved many very much. In glory, Devin no longer had diabetes. He had no cares about kidneys. He could soar with the Angels. He was free. I still run into people who share a Devin story.

My most precious story happened the week before Devin died he ran into a high school friend and his new wife. He asked if they had a church home. When they said no he invited them to be his guest at his church on what turned out to be his last Sunday. They came and sat on the row behind Devin. He had a diabetic episode at church that last Sunday. It took EMT's 45 minutes to work on Devin. That event scared them to death. I heard they joined church the very next Sunday. The day after we celebrated Devin's life. What a powerful testimony. I am thankful Devin loved God. I know God loves him and me.

After church that last Sunday, when Devin felt better he was driving home. Driving? Yes, I know. Anyway, he circled the church and came back around one more time. His pastor said "Man you know you should not be driving." Devin smiled at him and several deacons standing there. He said, "I just had to come back and tell you I'll be seeing you around." What a profound statement. I could see the impact it made on each of those persons who shared the same story. Yes, son, we'll be seeing you around.

Devin's last act of witnessing and his smile is a lasting memory for all those who mourn his loss. My daughter's Kasha's church members still tells her how anointed they felt the service was. Devin's bio family told me their only concern was that Devin was a believer. On that day there was no doubt he was. In that fact they were truly happy. His stepdad's family had a picnic the next day to honor his memory. That blessed me so much and gave me peace. God certainly poured his anointing over us all.

Reflections

1. Forgiveness has a healing effect. Have you tried forgiving all those hurts around your situation?

2. Have you forgiven yourself about any unresolved issues?

3. Do you feel released from any negative feelings concerning your loved one?

4. If not what can you do to accomplish the release?

5. Write down the person's name and the hurt associated with the name.

6. Are you willing to let those hurts go?

7. Pray for each person and the hurt on your list.

8. If you don't feel released yet, keep praying for them until you do. We must lay everything on Gods' Altar. He will give you peace.

CHAPTER EIGHT - LORD LIFT ME UP

The Monday after Devin's home going, I had a full knee replacement surgery. The surgery was pre-arranged months before my mom died. There seemed no reason to postpone it. I was going to be sad anyway. I decided I would rather be healing in the body and the heart at the same time. My surgery was a success.

When I awoke the first day, off and on, I saw a different faces sitting guard over me. My lifelong friends were taking turns being a ministry of presence in my hours of need. I wasn't surprised. When the call about my need went out all of my friends responded. These same friends continually showed up to encourage me, pray for me and lift me up. One time I woke to see stepdad reading the newspaper. My Lord. What wonders does God perform.

The doctor took extra precautions when a nurse found Devin's obituary program on my table. The nurse asked who it was. I shared with the nurse that I had just buried my son. The nurse shared the word with all the staff. I had not considered that my state of the mind could help or hinder my healing. But I had the sympathy vote. The staff always entered my room with care and concern. They always made me feel cared for. What a community I had. The Chaplain came by often. The physical therapist spent extra time working with me. I could not have been cared for any better. They treated me like I was one of their own. I let them. In fact I needed the extra love.

The Interlude

As I lay there healing God began to minister to me. I began to pray, earnestly, sincerely, with clarity of thought. My prayers were off because the music in my heart was off key. My prayers were not yet natural. My music was unsure and uncertain. God gave me a word "Interlude". In music between each movement there is a planned rest that must happen. It is a pre-planned length of time. The Interlude exists for us to fully appreciate what happened before and what happens next.

In the times I feared I lost my music. I thought I lost my heart song. I felt I lost my praise to God. God had pre-planned the Interlude in my life. A period I could reflect on. I could evaluate where I came from. I could reconnect to God in an intimate way. Through the reconnection, I could find my way to the next level. That next level would require a faith walk. When I could not see the way, God would be my light. This faith walk requires Gods' revelation. I had to trust God. I had lean on him. I had to stay connected to him. I thank God for the understanding. I realized my song was still here. It was just resting. I was in the spiritual interlude of my life. God wanted to give me time for my head and my heart to catch up.

As I stepped out on faith, I began to recall all the hills and mountains God had brought me over. How each time I grew. I began to be open more and more to his will. I reached toward all of my faith resources. I began to understand how important self-care was in the process. I began to sing. No longer superficially in the natural. I began to sing spiritually out of the depths of my soul. My prayer life was new. It was vibrant and different. God was perfecting my notes.

My retirement medical insurance approved sixteen visits for grief therapy. I used every single visit. I realized that I had made some bad choices in my own life. I was resentful of the limitations Devin caused by not accepting responsibility for his own illness. I allowed it. I was dealing with underlying anger on some level.

Laughter Heals the Soul

One day out of the clear blue I was reminded of an incident with him that made me mad. I began to tell him off. As I fussed I cried. I threatened bodily harm to him, really? I demanded explanations. I gave ultimatums. Then something peculiar happened.

I laughed. I laughed uncontrollably. I was sitting in my car driving down the highway and I looked ridiculous. As reality set in that Devin was gone, I stopped laughing. I told him how much I loved him. Then came the tears, rivers of them. God was washing away my sorrow. I know God heard me. A peace beyond all understanding came over me. I knew in some way God was purging me of all things I needed to let go of. I did it. I let go of anger, frustration, hurts and open wounds of hurtful memories.

Input Equals Output

Healing is a process that doesn't happen overnight. It takes time and a lot of energy. The hole in your heart never goes away. I like to say "The Hole in Your Heart Club" is not one you want anyone to join. But it makes you a perfect candidate to help others going through the process.

God called me into church membership as a young woman. As the mother of a critically sick child I learned about God's healing. Then God called me to a closer relationship with him. I learned how to walk in faith. God called me to study his word deeper. I learned to apply his word to my daily life. God increased my Spiritual Gift of Teaching. I began to share his word with others.

God called me to preach. God used my voice to reach others. When I accepted the call to preach, God then gifted me with Mercy. I was called to serve his people in compassion. I didn't understand it while it was happening. I do understand it now. Every step, every fall taught me something new. I learned how to love others who traveled the road I had just passed through. What a revelation when

God showed me the even greater works he has in store for me. What a mighty God we serve!

God is not through with me yet. While working to finish my graduate education I found the Clinical Pastoral Education (CPE) program. In CPE, as a Chaplain Intern, I work in Crisis, Trauma, Grief and Loss at the very hospital that cared for my son. God knew even when I didn't the mission for my life. I am so thankful.

I still serve at my local church of 41 years. I am now a local preacher assisting my senior pastor. I returned to work fulltime in child warfare. Those years loving children in foster care added a new dimension to my purpose. In addition I work part-time as a on call per diem Chaplain as needed with a local healthcare and hospice agency. What I've learn about end of life care has given me new insight into death from the patients point of view. God keeps perfecting me. I feel no one should die alone. I see the beauty of life as my patients cross over.

I do more for God now than ever. I have accomplished much in my latter years. I understand Gods' promises about his latter rain. I plan to work until God shows me the next assignment. Someone asked me recently what will I do if my health begins to diminish? My answer to them, "If I can't preach I'll teach. If I can't teach I'll pray. If I can't pray I'll sing. If I can't sing I'll just wave my hand". I know that God will honor whatever I do in praise. I give all praise, honor and glory to God for teaching and developing me along the way. Thank you God for your teachable presence of the Holy Spirit moving on my behalf. Being a servant leader while providing compassion and prayer to others is the highest calling.

When Job prayed for his friends,
the LORD restored his fortunes. In fact,
the LORD gave him twice as much as before!
Job 42:10

My name is not Job, but I do have a Job mindset when it comes to prayer. Prayer is now the music of my life. Prayer is communication to God in its' highest form. Praying for others benefits you and the person you are praying for. I don't mind interceding for others. When heaven rejoices I want to rejoice as well. My life is still a work in progress.

God keeps lifting me up. In finding my purpose I found God's plan for my life. I use every experience as a resource. I have found my testimony in the midst of my test. Have you found your purpose? Have you inquired of the Lord? I asked God what do you want me to do for you? Look what God directed me to do. I can't praise him enough.

Reflections

In her book "On Death and Dying", Elizabeth Kubler-Ross developed the five stages of grief. The progression of the grief states are;

1. **Denial** – "I feel fine." Showing denial is a defense.

2. **Anger** – "Why me? It's not fair!"; "How can this happen to me?"; *"Who is to blame?"* These are misplaced feelings.

3. **Bargaining** – "Just let me live to see my children graduate."; "I'll do anything for a few more years." This is the hope to postpone or delay death.

4. **Depression** – "I'm so sad, why bother with anything?"; "I'm going to die so what's the point?" This is the understanding of the certainty of death and grieving needs to process.

5. **Acceptance** – "It's going to be okay."; "I can't fight it, I may as well prepare for it." This is coming to terms with mortality.

1. Can you identify with each stage?
2. Have you worked through all the stages?
3. Have you repeated any of the stages?
4. Recognizing where you are and where you need to be is part of the process. If you haven't taken the time to evaluate where you are, now would be a good time to start.

CHAPTER NINE - LEARNING TO HEAL

Understand, therefore,

that the Lord your God is indeed God.

He is the faithful God who keeps his covenant

for a thousand generations and lavishes his unfailing love

on those who love him and obey his commands.

Deuteronomy 7:9

My Grieving Heart

When the music began to flow, my prayer was bolder, steady and sure.   I am in tune to who I have become in Christ. I understand how God wants to use everything I have been through for His glory. I would love to say that I have overcome all those negative, dark, and lonely feelings when grief knocks at my door. I can't. I would love to say that it doesn't bother me when I "attend a death" or make a "death visit" as the Chaplain, Pastor or friend. I can't. What I can say is that even when the music stops, I know God can still hear the song my heart wants to sing. I do believe those are the groaning's that the Holy Spirit utters on my behalf.

I encourage you to be realistic about your experiences in crisis, trauma, grief and loss. Human suffering happens to us all. The Adversary, the enemy of God is in charge of such things. While God doesn't cause suffering, he perfects us while we are going through it. Remember even Jesus wept with compassion for us.

Crisis, Trauma, Grief and loss feelings attack us unexpectedly. We go into high anxiety mode. Survival instincts kick in. We grieve as a process through life and death struggles. When death actually happens around and to us, we are not prepared. We have heart stopping no music moments. We might have Deja' vu moments of grief. Don't set limits or unattainable expectations at this time. Ask your questions. Work through your grief.

I can say I am a survivor. I survived the Oklahoma City Bombing in the loss of my younger cousin. What an incomprehensible loss. I survived the death of my sister. I had to go on for the sake of her 5 year old son. I survived the multiple deaths in 2006 of my Mother, my cousin and my Son. When death comes in waves of grief you just have to put one foot forward, step by step to make it happen. I also survived the loss of many other loved ones over the years. Many of my loved ones I thought God I'm not ready for them to go. Still I live on. No one is immune to death. If it hasn't happened to you keep living it will. This is not our eternal home. We all must die.

When my journey started I was the emotional one. I was the person no one wanted to sit by at the funeral. Yes, I would cry rivers of tears and be overly dramatic. As I lived, I learned. Death is not the end but a new beginning for those leaving. Death taught me to celebrate life while I can, in every way I can.

Certainly there are obstacles to overcome. The first obstacle is the fear of death itself. The next hurtle is the fear of the dying process. The fear of the unknown. We wonder what's on the other side. As humans we have to consider what resources are available. What is your faith resource?

In working with crisis, trauma, grief and loss, I encounter the full range of the human heart. I 've ministered from the atheist to those ready to meet their Lord. Every experience teaches me something new about crisis, trauma, death and loss. I also am reminded how human I am. I've learned to walk the last mile with others withdrawing from this life. I've learned to listen to the song their heart wants to sing, the words they want to share, the love they want to leave with us. Even if they could return many would not want to.

Death presents a new normal for those who are left behind. We are the ones who must work our way through our grief. We have to express our feelings. We have to maintain a normal life through the grieving process. We have to let our faith sustain us. We have to let our community in. We have to let go if and when it's time to do so. Have you let go yet?

Dealing with your loss is a process.
- From this moment on there is a hole in your heart.
- Healing doesn't happen overnight.

- Give yourself permission to grieve. Get it out.

- Spiritual time outs happen.

- There are times it takes all you have just to get from moment to moment.

- You find yourself praying your way through.

- You need quiet times just you and God.

- People say and do the wrong things. Let them off the hook.

- Some things you keep and some things you throw away.

- Look honestly at your feelings.

- Work through feelings of guilt, anger or betrayal as real as you can. It will be painful and your emotions will be raw but do it.

- Tell people what you need and want or don't need and don't want. Those who love you are waiting for you to direct them.

Have you told your loved ones what you need to just in case you or they leave too? The death reality doesn't end there.

- We have to work through the anniversaries, the holidays, the family gatherings, and the missing man formation at the dinner table.
- Honor yourself.
- Honor your loved one.
- Honor your loved ones story.
- Honor your memories.
- Honor your relationship with your loved one.
- Honor the life you shared.
- If you believe, Honor the God who gave you life.

Have you started honoring your loved ones life? What do you want to teach others about them? What do you want to teach others about you?

Re-engage with others:

- Remember to reach out when you are ready.
- Loneliness can be overpowering.
- Let others help you.
- Don't rush in but ease back into activities and social settings as you can.

- Someone I know still reminds me to: Don't would, could or should on yourself.
- Have no regrets.
- It is what it is and there is nothing you can do to change it.

People are your lifeline right now. Have you reached out to them? Let them back in quickly. Let them love you.

Prayer is an Option

When you can't find your own words to pray, the Lord's prayer is a good place to start.

The LORD is my shepherd; I have all that I need.
He lets me rest in green meadows;
he leads me beside peaceful streams.
He renews my strength.
He guides me along right paths,
bringing honor to his name.
Even when I walk through the darkest valley,
I will not be afraid, for you are close beside me.

Your rod and your staff protect and comfort me.

You prepare a feast for me in the presence of my enemies.

You honor me by anointing my head with oil.

My cup overflows with blessings.

Surely your goodness and unfailing love will pursue me

all the days of my life,

and I will live in the house of the LORD forever.

Psalm 23 A psalm of David

Have You Started Praying Yet?

When possible let God walk you through your valley experience. God is ready, willing and able to lift you up. Trust that his promises are true. His love for you is real. His loving kindness and his tender mercies are new for you every minute of every day.

- Pray to God about your pain, your heartache and your feelings of being alone. God will show up in unexpected ways.
- Take time to take care of you.

- Take things slow. Even if you hurry, healing doesn't happen any faster.

- Love on you every chance you get.

- Honor your Sabbath Rest. It's healing for a wounded soul.

Do you offer compassionate care to those you know are hurting? Allow God to use what you've been through. Share your own experience. Remember to tell your story. In the telling there is restoration. There is also revelation of things you might still need to deal with to heal.

Reflections

1. Are you feeling stuck in your grief?

2. Have you considered formal grief counseling?

3. What would stop you from considering counseling as an option?

4. Do you have other resources to help you work through your grief?

5. Would you seriously consider using them?

CHAPTER TEN - FINDING YOUR PURPOSE

Understanding human suffering in crisis, trauma, grief and loss is not for the faint of heart. It takes courage to deal with emotions. Death is an in your face assault on your body, mind and spirit that comes in never ending waves. It is sudden and brutal. It causes an instanteous physical reaction to all of your senses. Death has no mercy.

Your physical body is so reactive it can't handle or contain all the news you've just heard. Grief is hard. Doubt creeps in. This is not real; at least that's what your mind tells your heart. It's not true; because your eyes can't conceive your loved one not breathing in front of you. It didn't happen; because your brain can't absorb the floodgates full on with stimuli to the brain. They're lying to you; because these people don't know you. They don't know what you've been through. They don't know your story. Any minute someone will tell it's a joke or you're dreaming. Every fiber of your being is on overload.

Professionals call that "Grief". All you know is that it's painful and you want the pain to stop. If you have experienced the loss of a loved one then this book is for you. I found my purpose in sharing my story with you.

Opening the Floodgates

Then, when our dying bodies have been transformed
into bodies that will never die, this Scripture will be
fulfilled:
"Death is swallowed up in victory.
O death, where is your victory?
O death, where is your sting?"
For sin is the sting that results in death,
and the law gives sin its power.
But thank God!
He gives us victory over sin and death
through our Lord Jesus Christ.
So, my dear brothers and sisters,
be strong and immovable.
Always work enthusiastically for the Lord,
for you know that nothing you do for the Lord
is ever useless.

1 Corinthians 15:54-58

This passage of scripture speaks to the transformation of the body. It is a change from the physical to the spiritual. Often recited at funerals most times the words are drowned out by sorrow. This not the Apostle Paul's intention. His focus is on victorious living.

In the emotional battle between the heart and the mind we can't always appreciate the questions he asks. The full power of his statements become evident in the second part; "be strong, immovable!" Once the floodgates of emotion wash over us remember the admonition to be strong. Plant those feet and brace yourself.

Take Care of You

Death has many challenges. It brings multiple complications to the surface. It has many manifestations. Through grief we recognize the power of death and how powerless we become in the midst of it. Grief may cause significant physical symptoms, psychological distress and spiritual distress.

The Physical manifestations of grief are: loss of appetite, changes in weight, trouble falling asleep or staying asleep, fatigue, chest pain, headache, heart palpitations, hair loss and gastrointestinal distress. Grieving people are at increased risk for health problems and death.

The Emotional/Psychological manifestations of grief range from: sadness, anxiety, helplessness, emotional swings, irritability, apathy, disbelief, impaired concentration, lowered self-esteem, hallucination that the deceased person is present (visual or auditory), feelings of unreality, numbness, denial, searching for the deceased, flashbacks, suicidal thoughts, or depression.

The Spiritual effects of grief can become so crushing that you are thrown into a spiritual crisis. You may challenge or question your faith or religious beliefs. You may be angry at your God, or feel that life is empty and has no meaning. Why did God let this happen? Was there some purpose for it? Was this a part of God's plan? What reason could He have to allow a senseless death or suffering?

Is God punishing me? Why? Why? Why? Sometimes there aren't any reasons that would answer any of these questions. If you've experienced pain in this way, I hope you were encouraged by my story.

This book began in a desire to understand my own journey through personal crisis, trauma, grief and loss. As I began to look back over my life I could see the hand of God intervening consistently. Every stage of spiritual growth included mountain highs and valley lows.

For my purpose, how God dealt with me in human suffering was a pivotal revelation. The idea was no longer abstract. This happened to me. I hurt. My heart was broken. I began to remember the message of Ecclesiastes Chapter three; everything has a time.

God gave me free will. I decide which direction by my own choices. It is Gods' role to spiritually conduct the music in my life. He plans the structure; the highs, the lows and even the rests. God has a vision for my life from start to finish. I can't see what he sees or know what he knows but I trust what he tells me to do and when.

I am who I am called to be. I am the sum total of where I have been and what I have been through. I am at the appointed time and the appointed place in my faith walk. I choose to walk in the path God has ordained for me.

As Christians we exhale what we inhale. In other words we can't change what we haven't experienced. We can't share God's love without engaging with God's people. You can't empower loving from the side lines of life. You must get in the game.

When bad things happen you need to use all your resources. No one walks alone. God does his best to love us through our sufferings. He knows our human limitations, he made us. He loves us in spite of ourselves.

My prayer is that this book will empower and inspire those who are grieving. My journey speaks to all who mourn in general and to the Mother's nurturing spirit in particular. My ministry is one of compassionate presence. I follow the nudging of the Holy Spirit. My continued desire is to minister to those are still hurting.

My hope is that I have encouraged you through the telling of my successes and failures. My mission is to provide spiritual care to those needing spiritual resources. It's about moving toward healing through restoration, resolution and everything dealing with crisis, trauma, grief and loss.

Heaven Is Our Forever Home

Be blessed. Storms come to everyone at any time. God's word says that he rains on the just and the unjust. Sometimes the rain changes from a gentle rain to a downpour. Don't be discouraged, there is still life and healing in the water. Let me leave you with the passage of scripture that keeps me going day by day.

Paul's Prayer for Spiritual Growth

When I think of all this, I fall to my knees and pray to the Father, the Creator of everything in heaven and on earth. [I pray that from his glorious, unlimited resources he will empower you with inner strength through his Spirit. Then Christ will make his home in your hearts as you trust in him. Your roots will grow down into God's love and keep you strong. And may you have the power to understand, as all God's people should, how wide, how long, how high, and how deep his love is. May you experience the love of Christ, though it is too great to understand fully. Then you will be made complete with all the fullness of life and power that comes from God.

Now all glory to God, who is able, through his mighty power at work within us, to accomplish infinitely more than we might ask or think. Glory to him in the church and in Christ Jesus through all generations forever and ever! Amen.

Ephesians 3:14-21

All of heaven sings praises to God. Music is vital to our praise. Music has its' own healing power. I learned to use music to heal my grief. If a song was too sad, I played it over and over until it no longer invoked those bad feelings. I took negative associations to the music and replaced them with positive thoughts and memories. I began to listen without changing the channels or changing the songs.

When it comes to prayer, I prayed for all those things that hurt. I prayed for all those people who injured me. I prayed to forgive. I prayed often. I prayed a lot. It didn't take long before it didn't hurt as much anymore. I don't know what you will need to work through your grief, but find your own pattern and use it. There is no one correct way. I want to share with you my Thank You's. They were part of my healing process.

Devin's Family Acknowledgement

The family of Devin Todd Hamilton wishes to thank each of you. What a wonderful problem God has blessed us with having more churches available to us than we could use. More ministers to lift us up. More saints of God to pray us through Devin's home going.

Special thanks to the Oklahoma City Fire Department Station No. 15. You went above and beyond to serve in your rescue efforts each and every time you responded to an emergency call to "Devin's House". We thank you for the care and concern you always gave to Devin's son and daughter while you administered emergency care to Devin.

To the staff of the dialysis center at Deaconess Hospital who worked faithfully three times each week to keep Devin going. When Devin was late you always called to check on him. Sometimes those wake up calls at 5:00 am in the morning were the difference between life and death. To the angels of mercy God sent in Doctors Modhi Gude and Aly E. Aly, we appreciate you for your constant vigilance over Devin.

To the many saints of God we can never forget the countless days and nights you endeavored to pray for us. For that we will always feel blessed. Be encouraged for God is yet able to keep us according to our faith. You are the spiritual roots God gave us. Stay rooted and grounded in the Lord and keep looking up. The Family of Devin T. Hamilton Sr.

Reflections

1. What faith traditions religion did your family practice when you were growing up?

2. Did you learn your faith traditions from your parents or others?

3. Do you currently practice a faith tradition?

4. Do you believe in God?

5. What have been your important experiences and thoughts about God?

6. How would you describe Gods' role in your life?

7. Is it personal or impersonal?

8. Is it loving or stern?

9. Are you where you expected to be concerning God in your life?

10. What was the pivotal experience that helped or hindered you? Describe.

11. Jesus Wept. What does that mean concerning your life?

12. Jesus Saves. What does that mean concerning your future?

ABOUT THE AUTHOR

Debra L. Spears has seen first-hand the effects of trauma, crisis, grief and loss in her life and her role as friend, Mother, Foster Mom, Chaplain and Minister. She retired with 30 years' service from Southwestern Bell Telephone Company. Debra opened her home as an Emergency Foster Home (EFC). For 2 years she nurtured one teenager and 50 children under age 5.

Debra gave much to many. In grief, she focused on self-care. She also used her resources in grief counseling to heal. In 2011, Debra accepted her call to preach the Gospel. Highly motivated to become a better servant leader, Debra completed her Bachelor of Science Degree in Church Ministries and Master of Arts Degree in Leadership both at Mid-America Christian University.

God still has plans for her life. Debra returned to work in 2013 in child welfare. She was led to specialized ministry in Clinical Pastoral Education (CPE). In CPE Debra found her true Gift of Mercy in Pastoral Care. Debra is completing her Graduate work in Ministry. She functions as Local Preacher assisting at her home church of 41 years. She continues to serve as Chaplain Intern at the hospital and On Call Chaplain with a local health care & hospice. Debra remains thankful for God's purpose and God's plans for her life.

Thank you for purchasing this book. You may contact Debra by email at debralspearsbooks@gmail.com or at HULministries@aol.com. Also try me on my fan page at His Unveiled Love Ministries by Minister Debra L. Spears on Facebook.

"For the Lord your God...is a mighty Savior. He will take delight in you with gladness. With His love He will calm all your fears. " Zephaniah 3:17

Made in the USA
Charleston, SC
12 February 2015